THE CHURCH
IN THE
WORLD
NOT OF IT

PAUL STENHOUSE, MSC PhD

'IT WILL NOT BE IRRELEVANT TO EXAMINE THE
ANCIENT TRADITION AND THE DOCTRINE AND
FAITH OF THE CATHOLIC CHURCH WHICH, AS WE
KNOW, THE LORD HANDED DOWN, THE
APOSTLES PREACHED AND THE FATHERS
PRESERVED. FOR ON THIS TRADITION THE
CHURCH IS FOUNDED, AND IF ANYONE
ABANDONS IT, HE CANNOT BE A CHRISTIAN NOR
HAVE ANY RIGHT TO THE NAME.'
- ST ATHANASIUS OF ALEXANDRIA 296-373 AD

CHEVALIER PRESS
KENSINGTON NSW AUSTRALIA
1996

A *Chevalier Press* book, published by the
Missionaries of the Sacred Heart of Issoudun,
1, Roma Avenue Kensington NSW 2033
Australia

First published in June 1996
Distributed by Chevalier Press,
P.O. Box 13, Kensington NSW 2033 Australia.
Phones: *Australia* (02) *from outside Australia* (61-2)
662-7894/662-7188. Fax: 662-1910.

ISBN 0 86940 160 2

Cover photo and design: Paul Stenhouse, MSC
Formatting of art work: Gershwin Luhur.
Colour separations: David Graphics Sydney (02) 319 3700.
Printed in Australia by University of New England Press.

WE live in a world that is hostile to Catholicism and to Christianity. This hostility of the 'world' is predictable, since without what the French philosopher Maurice Blondel (1861-1947) called 'the eyes of faith' - a predisposition or opennesss to the possibility of supernatural truth - it seems that the gift of faith eludes 'worldly' people. Just as it eluded many of our Lord's contemporaries who had him tortured and put to death, despite, as St Peter put it, 'the miracles, portents and signs that God worked among you through him, as you well know.'[1]

Less predictable and more saddening is the frankly bitter hatred which so many so-called 'Christians,' who *flaunt* their faith in Jesus Christ, bear the Catholic Church and her teachings.

Part of the explanation for this widespread ignorance of Catholicism lies in the fact that many of our fellow Australians who seek the truth about Christianity, know little beyond the distorted images filtered through unsympathetic media, or through their various bible classes and Sunday Schools.

It may help to clear the air if we look at the Church as she really exists in this world, and then examine some of the criteria that have for the past two thousand years led people into Christ's Church, and back into it if, for whatever reason, they separated themselves for a time from the sheep-fold of Christ.

The Church and the World

Our Lord, in St John's gospel, warned us that there would always be conflict between the world and his Church. Shortly

---

[1] *Acts* ii,22.

1

before his Passion, Jesus prayed: 'The world hates them (his apostles and disciples) because they are strangers in the world, as I am. I pray thee, not to take them out of the world, but to protect them from the evil one.'[2]

Losing sight of our Lord's warning that we are meant to be 'strangers in the world,' many critics of the Church have blamed her for not working harder to procure material well-being for people (especially in third world countries). They seem not to know or care that for almost two thousand years the Catholic Church has worked tirelessly, tending to the spiritual and material needs of mankind.

Yesterday the descendants of those who wouldn't listen to her when she tried to warn them, blamed her for not stopping the First and Second World Wars.

Today she is blamed for poverty throughout the world, because she won't condone contraception and abortion; yet the truth is, as some sociologists are willing to point out, that overpopulation *in itself* is not the cause of poverty. Holland is the most densely populated country in the world and has little poverty. *Politics* is a major factor contributing to poverty in third world countries: roads and infrastructures need to be built from major centres to outlying villages and towns to enable crops to be moved and basic services, including jobs, to be set up.

The Catholic Church, almost single-handedly, has led and still leads the fight against social injustice. But not at the price of ignoring doctrinal and moral issues. And now, as throughout the whole of her two thousand years of existence, she is often ill-served by some of her members who like some politicians, doctors and lawyers, are deluded into attempting to treat *symptoms* and not *causes*.

---

[2] xvii,16,17.

2

Coming to terms with the world is far from easy for a dedicated Christian. And when that world is blatantly unjust and cruel, the Christian response is even harder to fine-tune.

'Liberation Theology,' to take but one example well known, at least by name, to most of us, was an attempt by dedicated and concerned Catholics, both clerical and lay, to resolve the timeless dilemma faced by Christians confronted by naked evil. It arose in Latin America as a response by mainly foreign missionaries to the deplorable political and social injustices endemic there.

As even non-religious commentators have pointed out, however, while it may have been a noble endeavour in many ways, it was fatally flawed. It applied already discredited Marxist theories to Christianity, and turned Catholic theology upside down by blaming poverty and social evils on abstract ideas like 'Market Forces,' or 'Free Trade' rather than on the innate sinfulness of individual men and women.

It also ignored the catastrophic evils unleashed on the world by Marxists/Leninist theories of socialism and the inherently atheistic and materialistic roots of communism.

The Catholic Church's position regarding institutionalised injustic is clear. She has condemned 'A theory that makes profit the exclusive norm and ultimate end of economic activity.'[3]

She deplores the 'disordered desire for money that cannot but produce perverse effects and is one of the many causes of the social conflicts that afflict our world'.[4]

---

[3] *Catechism of the Catholic Church*, ed. St Pauls, 2424.
[4] *Ibid.*

Subordinating the basic right of individuals and groups to the collective organisation of production is, in the teaching of the Catholic Church 'contrary to human dignity'. Any system that reduces persons to 'nothing more than a means of profit enslaves man, leads to idolising money and contributes to the spread of atheism'.[5]

The Catholic Church has rejected the totalitarian and atheistic ideologies associated in modern times with 'communism' or 'socialism'. She has likewise refused to accept, in the practice of capitalism, individualism and the absolute primacy of the law of the market place over human labour. Regulating the economy solely by centralised planning perverts the basis of social bonds. Reasonable regulation of the market place and economic initiatives in keeping with a just scale of values and a view to the common good, is to be commended.'[6]

Described as a 'quick fix' movement, 'Liberation Theology' has been criticised for being better at organising seminars, filling bookshelves and graves, than churches'.[7] Certainly many thousands of innocents have died in its name, including many fine priests and religious who could be ill spared from the spiritual role for which they were ordained and commissioned by the Church.

In the process, the spiritual lives of millions of people have been neglected in well-meant but ill-advised attempts to change political and economic systems, often by force: to save bodies, rather than souls; to fill bellies rather than minds and hearts. Priests have become involved with communist guerilla movements. Parishes have been turned into support networks for marxist rebels, priests and religious have exchanged their soutanes and religious habits for uniforms and been killed in battles with the oppressors.

---

[5] Ibid.
[6] Catechism of the Catholic Church, ed.cit. 245.
[7] The Weekly Telegraph, Feb.14-20, 1996: Ambrose Evans-Pritchard, 'Pope pays price of Latin Reformation,' p.20.

In the world, but not of it

The Church in the world has a paradoxical role: to be in the world, but not of it. The promoters of 'Liberation Theology' will tell you that there seemed no point in preaching salvation in a future heaven, while families suffered such grievous injustices here on earth. Yet the Church, while condoning the moderate use of force by the proper authorities, when appropriate to right wrongs, has never approved of priests and religious taking up arms and using the world's weapons against it - however attractive a short-term option that may appear.

Our Lord himself refused the mantle of political Messiah so anxiously desired by the Jews, suffering under the oppression of the Romans.[8] Jesus did not send his apostles out to lay seige to the world in a material sense, but to change it by bringing love and forgiveness and a sense of the value of suffering, to those who lived in it.

He did not rant against slavery, or against the Romans: he insisted that Peter pay the tax for the both of them. He did not send his apostles out to fight a guerilla war against the Romans, like the followers of the 'Son of the Star' - Bar Kochbar - the false messiah who led his people to destruction: he rather said to his apostles, 'I appointed you to go out and to bear fruit; fruit that will last: so that the Father may give you whatever you ask in my name. This is my command to you: love one another.'[9]

It may make no sense to the editor of the *Wall Street Journal*, or the pundits in the London School of Economics, for a priest to die along with his people, while encouraging and

---

[8] *John* vi,15; *Acts* i, 6-7.
[9] *John* xv, 16,17.

supporting them through peaceful means to achieve their goals of justice and equality.

The Catholic Church, however, has praised those 'who renounce violence and bloodshed, and in order to safeguard human rights make use of those means of defence available to the weakest.'[10] Such people 'bear witness to evangelical charity provided they do so without harming the rights and obligations of other men and societies. They bear legitimate witness to the gravity of the physical and moral risks of recourse to violence, with all its destruction and death'.[11]

But paradoxically, the result, according to *secular commentators*, of the politicisation of Catholicism in Latin America through the Marxist-style 'Liberation Theology' has been a violent physical backlash by the military dictatorships, and an equally disastrous spiritual reaction against the Catholic Church on the part of the poor.

Filling the Void

With fewer priests to do the pastoral work, the poor Catholic flock has been laid waste, and lies exposed to the wolves - the anti-Catholic Protestant fundamentalists - mainly from America - who have filled the void, clutching their bibles and broadcasting through loudspeakers their message of 'salvation,' - only this time a priestless and Churchless 'salvation' - vastly different from that which should have been preached by the pastors of the flock.

Now, anti-Catholicism has taken the field, wearing the same colours as the socially unjust politicians and the exploiters of the poor. The Catholic Church finds herself once again weakened by the efforts of her own well-meaning but reckless followers who seem to have forgotten our Lord's warning: 'If

---

[10] *Catechism of the Catholic Church*, 2306.
[11] *Ibid.*

6

you belonged to the world, the world would love its own; but because you do not belong to the world, because I have chosen you out of the world, for that reason the world hates you. Remember what I said, "A servant is not greater than his master." As they persecuted me, so they will persecute you; they will follow your teaching as little as they followed mine. It is on my account that they will treat you thus: because they do not know the One who sent me.'[12]

Many well-meaning Catholics of limited vision, who rightly insist on 'listening to the voices' of the poor and the socially diasadvantaged, strangely ignore the voices of those in authority in the Church, especially the Supreme Pontiffs who not only are equally concerned for social justice, but actually invented the term. Too many concerned Catholics who agonise over the injustices that afflict them and their people have forgotten that, despite contrary opinions, God's voice is *not* to be heard in the strong wind, or the earthquake or the fire, or the AK47 or the mortar shell, but in 'a still, small voice'.[13]

Struggling with the Paradox of the Church

There are those, in Australia and elsewhere, who struggle to *immerse the Church in the world* as if thereby they may gain its favour, and appear more relevant to the media and to their non-believing friends. Such attempts at compromise with the world have always been the greatest temptation facing priests and religious since Satan tried to seduce our Lord in the wilderness, and Judas betrayed him for thirty pieces of silver.

In some countries 'New Age' types empty the seminaries with their un-Catholic teaching, and refuse to encourage vocations among the young, and at the same time promote divisive issues like the ordination of women and 'choice' in all moral

---

[12] *John* xv, 19-21.
[13] *1 Kings* xix,13

7

areas, especially the draw-cards of contraception, abortion and euthanasia. Giving people what they want may well be the misguided role of politicians; it should not be the goal of Christians whose *raison d'etre* is to help people rise about their 'wants' to recognize, like Francis Thompson, that true happiness lies elsewhere.

Others struggle *to take the Church out of the world altogether*; retiring into a different 'world' of self-delusion, private interpretation, visions, 'tongues' and prophecies, of so-called 'spirit' - the unreal and self-contradictory world beloved of the early Gnostics, the Calvinists, Jansenists, Puritans, so-called 'ecstatic faiths,' and modern-day fundamentalists.

Like St Peter who cut off Malchus's ear trying to prevent Jesus being taken by the soldiers of the High Priest, these imagine that they can save themselves and the world by taking our Lord down from his cross. 'Sheathe your sword,' our Lord told him, 'this is the cup the Father has given me; shall I not drink it?'[14] 'In very truth I tell you, you will weep and mourn, but the world will be glad. But though you will be plunged in grief, your grief will be turned into joy.'[15]

Belief and trust in this joy, which will be the reward of those who persevere out of love, is what separates true faith in the Church that our Lord founded, from the spurious faith of many vocal proponents of force and violence in the name of justice; or of retreat from the world into a kind of spiritual Disneyland where puppets and special effects dazzle the eyes, and paralyse the will. No one pretends that arriving at belief in this joy and the ultimate victory of good over evil, or that persevering in it, is easy: but there is no alternative open to the true follower of Christ.

---

[14] *John* xviii, 10,11.
[15] *John*, xvi,20.

8

This should now be obvious to those priests and religious who joined the ranks of the *Sandinistas* in Nicaragua. In 1979 they overthrew by violent means the oppressive US backed regime of Somoza in the Central American Republic. Having thrown off their religious garb and donned the politician's suit they betrayed their fellow-countrymen and the Church in a fashion that makes a mockery of the slogans that ushered in their much vaunted 'New Age'.

Which Church Qualifies for the Title?

The true Church of Christ can be recognized in this world of hi-tech warfare, credit cards, the internet and trial by media devoted, body and soul, to 'entertaining' the world at no matter what cost, by her fidelity to the Deposit of Faith, to the Tradition of the apostles; by her refusal to take the extreme course; by her willingness to compromise, when compromise is possible. Against all odds, she refuses to sell her old lamp that is 'the light of the world,' for the latest fashion in religious light fittings.

In principle Christ's Church is un-fashionable. She can be recognised by her loyalty to the Apostolic Tradition, to Mary the mother of Jesus, and to her beloved dead, 'who sleep in Christ'[16] down through the ages. She protects the unborn as well as the young, the aged and the the infirm. She remains the same - from the catacombs to the third millennium.

Like her master she sits and eats with sinners. She is not scandalised by sin; only by the unrepentant sinner. For she has the answer to sin; and a power over it that is the envy of angels and men. She is condemned for her concern for sinners; and often ridiculed for being so forgiving. Her enemies should not forget the ominous implications of that part of the Our Father where we pray to God that he will

---

[16] *Missale Romanum*, Roman Canon, prayer for the dead after the Consecration.

forgive us exactly as we have forgiven others.[17] To be unforgiving, is to risk being eternally unforgiven.

Like her Master, the Church that Christ founded speaks with authority and meets with ridicule and abuse for doing so. Our generation is not the first to have baulked at submitting to authority. But it may well go down in history as the first to have ended by rejecting all authority other than that of the so-called 'individual conscience'. The final Act in the drama conceived by Martin Luther.

Like her master, the Church that Christ founded is hauled before judges and condemned for speaking the truth. Almost all religious and secular 'leaders' hold her up to ridicule, for refusing to be seduced by criticism or praise. The Pope is condemned for not allowing the media, and vociferous lobbyists inside and outside the Church, to set the *agendum* for the Church.

Like her Master, the Church of Christ finds that many walk with her no longer, because they have found her teaching hard. She and we should expect nothing less. Like her Master, she has been betrayed by friend and foe alike. Like her Master, she has done good, and been damned for it; worked miracles, and her enemies have conspired to destroy her. That they will not succeed we know from our Lord's promise that 'the gates of hell will not prevail against her'.[18] But that doesn't lessen the pain.

In Australia, for example, she expends almost all her worldly possessions on Catholic Education. Too many of the secondary schools she runs, in the present climate of secularism and liberalism in morals and doctrine, have become nests of anti-Catholicism promoted by too many non-

---

[17] '... just as we forgive those who have trespassed against us'. *Matthew*, vi, 9.
[18] *Matthew*, xvi,18.

believing teachers who exploit the Church's goodness, and the State's indifference, for their own purposes.

From the arms of John, the beloved disciple, the Church that Christ founded received Mary, the mother of Jesus - the last bequest from her son dying on the cross. His Church can be recognised by her love and reverence for his mother Mary, the mother of all Christians.

1. The Church Must be Apostolic

We moderns, knowing too little of the past and brought up to believe in a Creed of self-promotion, and self satisfaction, at all times and at all cost, not unnaturally are attracted by teachers who encourage us to believe that what we think (or rather feel) is most important and that nothing is of greater importance. And this applies as much to religion and faith as it does to taste in food, clothing, cars or cosmetics.

Yet the fact that the true Church of Christ must be built, not upon the whims and feelings and wants of Christians, but upon the solid rock foundation of the teaching and authority of the apostles, is incontrovertible - for those with eyes to see and ears to hear.

Recently I interviewed a young man, formerly an Anglican, now a member of the Assemblies of God, who could see no need for any foundation for his faith other than his own personal acceptance of Jesus. He had no need for the Church, he said, because the bible was enough for him. His arguments will be discussed at length, later on in this series.

Where outside the Catholic Church whose head is the bishop of Rome, successor of St Peter, will you find Apostolic foundations in any of the churches that claim to be true vehicles for passing on the teachings of Jesus today?

Apostolic Sees?

None of the Orthodox Churches existing today, many of which are vociferously anti-Catholic, can claim *unbroken* fidelity to the apostolic teaching, or *unbroken* descent from the apostles. Of the original Apostolic Sees - Jerusalem, Antioch, Rome and Alexandria - the latter three were all regarded in the ancient Church as *Petrine* Sees, because Antioch and Rome were established by St Peter, and Alexandria was founded by St Mark, the disciple of St Peter - only the See of Rome, the Chair of Peter and his successors, can prove itself to have remained constantly faithful to the Tradition handed down by the Apostles.

The Apostolic See in Jerusalem, whose head was St James, no longer exists as such. And sadly, neither Antioch nor Alexandria kept free from heresy, and broke their links with Apostolic succession.

Constantinople, the old Byzantium, the nominal head of the Orthodox Churches, was not founded by an apostle. When it was still the old port of Byzantium, Christians had gathered there from the second century; but its bishop was always subject to the bishop of Heraclea Pontica, in Thrace.

For political reasons, after Byzantium became Constantinople and the capital of the Eastern empire, attempts were made to elevate Constantinople to a Patriarchate, subordinate to Rome in its Catholic primacy over the Universal Church, but superior in honour to the Sees of Antioch, Alexandria and Jerusalem.

The first attempt was at the Council of Constantinople in 381 AD (by a canon, 3, that was never ratified by Rome and became a dead letter) and the second occurred after the Council of Ephesus broke up in 451 AD by a few politically minded bishops favourable to Constantinople (by canon 28, that was refused ratification by Pope St Leo the Great in 451

AD). Constantinople lost all claim to apostolicity when it broke its communion with the See of Rome in 1054. The link was reforged temporarily at the Council of Florence when Constantinople sought re-union with Rome for political purposes (the Turks were at the gates of the city) but the act of Union was never promulgated.

Alone in the world, the Church of Rome, founded on the twin pillars of St Peter 'the Rock,' and St Paul, 'the Apostle of the Gentiles,' can lay claim legitimately to be the true Apostolic Church founded by Christ. In the early Church *all* the Apostolic Churches - Jerusalem, Antioch, Rome and Alexandria - could be appealed to as a test of Orthodoxy. But the Church of Rome, even then, as we learn from St Irenaeus of Lyons (130-200), Tertullian (160-220) and St Augustine (354-430) would be appealed to at any time, by all other Churches, not just because she was *de facto* Apostolic, like some of the others, but because she was the pre-eminent Apostolic Church: Apostolic *de iure* because she was the See of St Peter, the Rock, upon which the Catholic Church was founded.

For almost a thousand years there has been no other Apostolic Church *except* the Church of Rome. She has a two-fold right to that privilege, and other Churches have a two-fold obligation to be in communion with her as the only means of establishing their own Apostolicity.

Valid Orders and Apostolic Succession

It may not be out of place to say something here about Apostolicity as it affects Anglicans and Lutherans, Old Catholics and others who confuse Apostolicity with *valid orders*, and *material continuity* in the Sees and Churches.

The fact that there has been an unbroken line of bishops of Canterbury, since Pope St Gregory the Great sent St Augustine to England in 596 AD, satisfies some Anglicans that their Apostolic succession is intact. Despite the fact that since the time of Henry VIII (with the exception of Cardinal Pole) all Archbishops of Canterbury and English bishops of the Church of England have had neither valid orders nor communion with Rome.

The question of the invalidity of Anglican Orders was decided by Pope Leo XIII's Bull *'Apostolicae Curae'* in 1896. But many Anglicans have sought ordination from Old Catholics and schismatic Orthodox bishops, thinking thereby to ensure their legitimacy.

This linking of *validity* of ordination with *Apostolicity* carries no weight at all. For was not the heretic Arius (250-336) a priest in Alexandria? Were not the Arian bishops in the fourth century validly ordained? Nestorius (died 451) and Appolinarius (310-390) were both validly ordained: they both occupied Sees of Catholic predecessors: Nestorius was bishop of Constantinople, and Apollonius was bishop of Laodicea on the Syrian coast.

It is not impossible that a validly ordained bishop may be a heretic in 1996. And what about schism? If heresy and schism destroy the Apostolicity of a bishop or a See and a particular Church, then clearly something more than *valid* orders or *material, local* continuity, is required.

What then is the condition for Apostolicity? According to Tertullian and St Augustine, it is *Communion with an Apostolic Church* whose Apostolic character is beyond question and whose line of bishops, from Apostolic times, is unbroken. As the Church of Rome alone possesses the quality of Apostolicity, communion with her is essential if Churches wish to form part of the Church that Christ founded.

All Protestant Churches lost the Apostolic link when they followed Martin Luther into heresy in the sixteenth century. Later on they were forced to deny the importance of such an

Apostolic link, claiming that *faith* was sufficient for them. This is flying in the face of tradition and fact, but it none the less remains the contention of such Churches today.

2. The Church must be One

Human beings are fascinated by unity. Perhaps because the DNA of all of us, and indeed of all living things (funghi excepted) is composed of the same four bases, our complex human nature seeks unity consciously and unconsciously. Even *destroyers* of unity, like Martin Luther, or Calvin, sought in their turn a perverse alternative kind of unity, based on *their own* idea of the Church. Just as home breakers who destroy a marriage often seeks to set up a new kind of union, based on *them* instead of the original partner.

The Catholic Church is One, in her divine head Jesus, and her earthly head, the bishop of Rome who is Christ's Vicar. Separating oneself from the Catholic Church will *diminish* that unity but not destroy it; will *tarnish* but not discredit it.

The Catholic Church is One, also, in her teaching. We should be able to find out *what* she teaches by asking any well-informed practising Catholic. Sadly, this may not be so easy today. But fortunately for the seeker-after-truth, Catholic faith is not measured by what an individual Catholic may claim to believe, but by the voice of the Church, expressed since Pentecost Day through her unwritten and written tradition, her Pontifical Decrees and Conciliar Acts. These are, collectively, the *litmus test*. To fail this test is not to destroy the Church's unity; only to withdraw from it with all the sad consequences that this implies.

St Paul cautions us to 'maintain the unity of the Spirit in the bond of peace,' for sin and its baneful consequences constantly threaten the gift of unity.

The Catholic Church is One, also, in her practice. No matter how diverse her members are they form part of the One Mystical Body of Christ, and their fidelity to her laws and practices, discipline doctrine and customs is something that she does through them. 'Look not on our sins,' we pray at Mass, 'but on the Faith of your Church'.

We are enfolded in the Church's arms. We do not lose our individuality when we embrace her: rather we become individual members of that One Body of Christ which is the Church. This diversity in Unity is a Mystery. St Augustine described it in terms of our being the little fish that follow Christ the Big Fish. St Ignatius of Antioch compared the individual Catholic to the little grains of wheat that go to make up the Bread that is the Body of Christ. Christ's Church remains a miracle of Unity because she is the Mystical Body of Christ, no matter how many of her members separate themselves from her.

3. The Church Must be Catholic

Many Protestant Christians use the term 'Catholic' very loosely and may even think of themselves as 'Catholic' without knowing anything of the true meaning of the term. Perhaps, subconsciously, they seek thereby to legitimise doctrines and practices that they know in their heart of hearts to be novel, un-Catholic and contrary to the Apostolic Tradition.

Whatever their reason may be, the truth is that until the schism of the Byzantines that split the Catholic Church in the eleventh century (1054) all Christians, who were truly such, were Catholic because they were in communion with the Successor of St Peter in the See of Rome, the Pope.

St Vincent of Lerins, who lived in a monastery on the island of that name off the coast of France near Nice, wrote a commentary against heretics in 434. In it he gives a broad definition of 'Catholic' faith: 'That which is everywhere, always and by everybody believed, is consequently truly and properly Catholic'.[19] He wrote six centuries before the beginnings of the 'Orthodox Church' and eleven hundred years before the appearance of Martin Luther.

That communion with the Church of Rome is synonymous with communion with the Catholic Church is made clear in a letter addressed to Antonianus, a bishop in Numidia, by Cyprian of Carthage (martyred in 258). 'You have written,' he wrote, 'that I should transmit to our colleague Cornelius (Pope of Rome 251-253) a copy of your letter in order that, laying aside all solicitude, he should know that you are in communion with him, that is, with the Catholic Church.'[20]

The Hebrew word for 'Catholic,' commonly used in the early centuries, was 'Eshkol' an acronym for four Hebrew words that mean: 'A person in whom there is everything'. The word refers not to inflated egos or 'know all' attitudes, but to the well-known fact that Christians who were Catholic paid no heed to tribe or language or culture or country.

This was a scandal to the Jews, and is today an aspect that still sets genuine Catholics apart from 'would be' ones. A true Catholic cannot be concerned only for those of his own social or national background. Catholics cannot be racists or xenophobic and still legitimately claim this proud title.

Those Jews who survived the destruction of Jerusalem would not allow non-circumcised Christian gentiles into the synagogue, leading to the exclusion of the Catholics from Jewish worship sometime around 110 AD. A prayer, 'cursed be the Minim' ('cursed be the heretics, i.e. the Christians') was added to the Eighteen Benedictions customarily said by

---

[19] 'Quod ubique, quod semper, quod ab omnibus creditum est, hoc est etenim vere proprieque *Catholicum*'.

[20] *Epistola* 52: 'Ad Antonianum: de Cornelii Papae ordinatione.'

17

the Jews who worshipped alongside Christians in the Synagogue until that time. It could not be said by the Jewish or Gentile Catholics, and they left the Synagogue, never to return. According to *Berakhot* 28b, Samuel ha-Katan introduced the prayer at the invitation of Gamaliel II of Jabneh. It was 'primarily directed against Judaeo-Christians'.[21]

The Roman Church: Truly and Alone Catholic

St Augustine (354-430) writing in 400 AD says, 'The very name 'Catholic' holds me in the Church - a name which, not without cause, amidst so many heresies, she alone has obtained. So that whilst all heretics wish to be called Catholic, should any stranger enquire of them where the Catholic Church is, none would dare point out their own house or church.'[22]

That the bishop of Rome is the successor of St Peter in that See was never denied by anybody until the time of the Protestant reformation in the sixteenth century. Towards the end of 376 St Jerome (born in Stridonium, in Hungary in 331, and died in 420) wrote to Pope Damasus,

> 'I have considered it my duty to consult the Chair of Peter. I speak with the successor of the fisherman, with the disciple of the cross. I, following no leader but Christ, am united in communion with your Blessedness, that is, with the Chair of Peter.'[23]

St Ambrose of Milan, speaking of the bishop of Rome, says: 'Where Peter is, there is the Church: and where the Church is, there is no death, but only eternal life. On that Rock I know that the Church was built'.

---

[21] *IQZ* 10(1897/1898). See *Encyclopaedia Judaica* vol 12 col3 par.2.

[22] See *The Chair of Peter*, by John Murphy, Burns and Oates, London. p.31 note 2.

[23] *Epistola* xv, *alias* lvii.

St John Chrysostom, one of the eminent Greek Fathers of the Church acknowledged that St Peter had jurisdiction over the whole world: 'Peter was pre-eminent among the apostles, the mouth of the disciples, the head of the assembly.'[24] Elsewhere[25] he wrote of Peter: 'He became the first of the disciples and the whole world was committed to him.'

The Voice of Pope Agatho is the Voice of Peter

None of the Orthodox Churches has ever dared deny to the Church of Rome the title 'Catholic' The Fathers of the Council of Carthage, in 416, wrote to Pope Innocent I asking him to confirm their condemnation of the British monk Pelagius: 'Lord Brother, we have deemed that this affair should be made known to your Blessedness so that the authority of the Apostolic See may be applied to our humble statutes, to secure the salvation of many as well as to correct the perversity of some.'[26]

Modern-day critics of the Primacy of St Peter and his successors are drawn mainly from Orthodox or Protestant communities, who understandably, try to justify their 'rejectionist' position and separation from communion with the See of Peter, and fly in the face of history and common sense. Lately these have been joined by former Catholics who have abandoned the Church's orthodox doctrinal and moral position, and wish, in their turn, like Martin Luther and all his descendants, to mollify their consciences by denying the Pope the authority to act contrary to their wishes and feelings.

Yet so convinced were all Catholics of East and West that the bishop of Rome was St Peter's successor and held pre-eminence over all other Sees that when the Byzantine emperor

---

[24] *In Johannem*, Homil. lxxxviii *alias* lxxxvii.

[25] *Adversus Judaeos* viii,3.

[26] Apud S. August. *Epistola* xc.

19

published a decree in 639 that Pope Agatho regarded as heretical, the emperor immediately withdrew it, wrote to the Council of Rome, praising the Pope as 'the universal Prince of Pastors' for the zeal with which they had defended the Catholic faith, and adds: 'We prized the words of Agatho as the voice of Blessed Peter himself'.[27]

None of the Protestant Churches, despite attempts by the use of the term 'Roman Catholic' - unknown until the reformation - to pretend that they too are Catholic (but not in the same way as the Church of Rome), has any possibility of legitimising its claim to the title.

4. The Church Must be Holy

Holiness has, for all her existence, been the characteristic, *par excellence*, of the Catholic Church. In recent times, in this country and elsewhere, we have had too many sad examples of the frailty of human nature not to be aware of our own sinfulness and the distance that separates us from the holiness to which we are called. Fortunately, the holiness of the Church does not depend upon us. It is we, who depend upon the holiness of the Church. She is holy because of her founder, who was no frail and imperfect human being, like the founders of the myriad heretical and schismatic sects that have arisen in opposition to her teaching and authority throughout her two thousand years. The names of some of the better known among them (and the sects they founded) follow:

Montanus (the *Montanists*, founded 172 AD), or
Donatus (the *Donatists*, founded c.311 AD), or
Arius (the *Arians*, founded 319 AD) or
Apollonius (the *Apollonians*, founded 362 AD) or
Pelagius (the *Pelagians* founded c.410 AD) or
Nestorius (the *Nestorians* founded 428 AD), or

---

[27] Baronius, *Annales*, viii, 559,560.

... Martin Luther (the *Lutherans*, founded 1517 AD), or
John Calvin (the *Calvinists*, founded 1533), or
Henry VIII (the *Church of England* founded 1534) or
John Knox (the *Presbyterians* founded 1560) or
Robert Browne (the *Congregationalists* founded 1580), or
John Trask (the *Seven Day Baptists* founded early seventeenth century)
James Nayley/George Fax (the *Quakers* founded in 1624) or
John Lothropp (the *Baptists* founded 1633) or
#John and Charles Wesley (the *Wesleyans/Methodists* founded in 1729).
.. Thomas Campbell (the *Christadelphians* founded 1809) or
Darby (the *Plymouth Brethren* founded in 1830) or
Miller (the *Adventists* founded in 1831) or
William Booth (the *Salvation Army* founded in 1861) or
Mrs Mary Baker Eddy (the *Christian Scientists* founded 1875) etc.

The founder of the Catholic Church was not St Peter, or St Paul, or any other of the Apostles. Her founder is our Lord, Jesus Christ. And what's more, the Catholic Church can *prove* it.

The Catholic Church is also holy in her teaching - whether those to whom it is preached accept it or not - in her Sacraments, in her laws, in her miracles, in her healing of soul and body, in her members. All who belong to her are called to holiness.

She is made up of many imperfect human beings, all attached to her in varying degrees of closeness; and she is all the holier for the attraction that she holds for those in need of her healing grace. Her holiness infuriates her foes, who love to point out instances of human fraility among her members. But unlike her critics (and unlike the media who feed off their prurient revelations) she rejects no sinner and her forgiveness in the name of Christ knows no bounds. All that she asks in return is true sorrow for sin and a true longing for holiness.

21

The true Church of Christ exists, today, in our world. She is the leaven in the mass, the city built on the mountain top, the mustard seed that grows into a giant tree, the net cast into the sea. Without knowing it, most Christians and many non-Christians are genuinely seeking her. You can recognize her from the scars she bears: from her crown of thorns and the wounds in her hands and feet; and the spear thrust in her side. She is the Body of Christ in our world.

Those who would abuse and slander this Catholic Church do so at their peril. Let the words of Gamaliel the Pharisee, addressed to the Sanhedrin in Jerusalem in the days succeeding our Lord's Ascension into heaven, almost two thousand years ago, give grounds for caution: 'Keep clear of these men; I tell you, leave them alone. For if this idea of theirs or its execution is of human origin, it will collapse; but if it is from God, you will never be able to put them down; and you risk finding yourself at war with God.'[28]

---

[28] *Acts* v, 38-39.